MW01195814

Coming Home

Be the Hero of Your Own Story
(regardless of previous chaos, choices and chapters)

KAREN NOVY

BALBOA.PRESS
A DIVISION OF HAY HOUSE

Balboa Press books may be ordered through booksellers or by contacting:

Balboa Press
A Division of Hay House
1663 Liberty Drive
Bloomington, IN 47403
www.balboapress.com
844-682-1282

Interior Artwork Credit: Karen Novy
Image Editing: Clara Spagnardi

Print information available on the last page

ISBN: 978-1-9822-7613-3 (sc)
ISBN: 978-1-9822-7615-7 (hc)
ISBN: 978-1-9822-7614-0 (e)

Library of Congress Control Number: 2021921532

Balboa Press rev. date: 12/29/2021

Contents

PART TWO

PART THREE

I dedicate this book to my children:
Clara and Fergus,
you are my teachers, and I am honored
to love and be loved by you.

Acknowledgements

For you, my dear reader:
May this book shed some light, be a guide, ignite the
spark that reminds you that there is infinite magic in
you and all around you, every moment of every day.

Thank you to everyone in my life who supports my journey,
my expansion. I appreciate your love and kindness as I walk
my path and evolve. I am grateful for you, and I hope that you
experience great abundance and love on your own journey.

Thank you to Turkey Land Cove Foundation for a two-week
writer's residency grant that launched this manuscript.

Thank you CJ Scarlet, Ann Jagger, and Nancy
Aronie for your encouragement.

A very special thank you to Cheryl Chamblee
(amazing person, poet, writer, editor, creator)
for helping to make this book even better.

PART ONE

HOMECOMING

Coming home to oneself
is the greatest experience
a human being can have.
Waking up to the profound idea
that you, and you alone,
are the master of your destiny
responsible for your happiness
free to choose your path
to dive inside yourself
and remember your very essence.
To celebrate your unique divinity
to pursue your life's dream
to realize your potential
to create where there was none
to accept each day as a gift,
a chance, an offering,
a precious and fleeting moment.
Listening to the voice,
the one that guides you
and has guided you
since before you can remember.
Resuming your wholeness
Reclaiming your joy
Returning to love
Homecoming

❧ The Call

"Yes... this is she," I answered.

"It is breast cancer," I heard her say.

My legs turned to rubber. "I'm sorry, what?"

I sat down. Everything began to move in slow motion, as though I was under water. How could I possibly have cancer? It didn't make sense.

I had subconsciously done everything in my power to stay under the radar, to keep myself safe and small, to resist pursuing my passion because, in my child-mind, that's why my dad died young. He left a career in sales to become a full-time musician and piano teacher and, five years later, he got sick. Cancer.

Everything I did (or perhaps more accurately avoided), all the decisions I made to resist my calling, to bury my heart, to shut down the music . . . that was all supposed to keep me *safe*.

Not so, it turns out. And that's when it hit me. Hard.

It's not at *all* the way I imagined. It's the exact opposite. It's not denying or fearing your powerful essence, but embracing it and fully stepping into your truth, that brings you health and happiness, that makes you whole.

I had fallen asleep at the wheel. I had suppressed my heart's desire for so many years, and there it was. A tumor, in my left breast, way back on the chest wall, right near my heart. The body knows. The body keeps score.

It was mid-June 2015. I grappled for weeks with how to move forward. Surgery, radiation, all the options. I did tons of research; I went for long walks to clear my head; I met with my team of oncologists to get all of my questions answered. My family, friends and neighbors all offered great love and support.

And then. Late June. The dragonflies:

I'm walking on a trail near my house, thinking, and dragonflies begin to circle around me. Not just a few. Many. They encircle me as I walk. They move with me. They silently speak to my heart. It is exactly in this moment that I know, without a shadow of a doubt, that I will survive. I will be okay. More than ok, in fact. Because I'm being given the ultimate opportunity, a second chance, to finally stop running and to embrace my truth, to bring my gifts, my light to the world in a big way.

After healing from surgery and radiation therapy, I began transforming in other areas of my life. These transformations are the silver linings of my breast cancer diagnosis. The Universe had been trying to get through to me for *so* long, and the only way I finally heard was in facing my mortality head on.

I am listening now. I hear that little voice.

✑ The Awakening

Sometimes that little voice has to yell to get your attention.

My breast cancer diagnosis was a wake-up call for me. The Universe was telling me to be authentic, to share my music, my light, my heart. Deeply and intentionally, I began exploring my life's purpose, what I really felt called to do; that which, out of fear and feelings of unworthiness, I had not pursued.

The knowing, the nudges, the intuition, the little voice—it got stronger the more attention I gave it. "Finally," I heard it say, "You're listening."

The ability to sit in stillness, to give ourselves time to undo the chaos and the noise of the day, to acknowledge our inner beauty and knowing, these are important gifts of time and intuition that we give ourselves. The stillness gives way to our divine essence, helps us to discern what really lights us up, and emboldens us to use the gifts that we embody to share more love and joy with the world.

✦ The Journey

I believe we all want to be happy and at peace, to feel a sense of contributing to the greater good, to have purpose. We all want to feel connected. We are more alike than we are different. It's so important that we follow our joy, and allow ourselves the freedom to be happy. To create our life, the way we want and know it can be. The best and highest version of our soul's expression in this lifetime. You know what it feels like to be in the flow, to be open to the joy and love that is within you. It feels really good: carefree, playful, childlike, liberating.

My hope is this: that we all give ourselves permission to dream beyond sleep, to believe even in the face of challenging circumstances, to see what is not yet to be seen in our physical reality with the naked eye. We owe ourselves and each other that much. We owe that to the world at large.

It serves no one to hide our light and hoard our gifts. We must share our light, the creative energy that is Source/Love. What I call the Big Love. We are all a part of the Whole, all playing a part in raising the vibration of the collective consciousness.

Part of the reason that my diagnosis—one of the defining moments in my journey—was so shocking was because I had believed, to that point, that playing small and safe would keep me from any risk or disaster.

As children, sometimes we take in information around us and then accept our beliefs about that (very likely) misleading or misinterpreted information. Then our beliefs, however misguided, become our reality and inform our perceptions. This, in turn, limits us from our real and highest potential and leads us to disconnect from our truth, and we go through the motions of existence. Surviving, not thriving. A linear rather than exponential existence.

I had turned my back on myself *so* many times, that I didn't even know which way I was facing, much less the direction to go. I was so disconnected from my truth, my real true inner being that knows who I am and what my purpose is. And once I started listening again – well, there is no un-hearing! The momentum starts rolling, and we return to ourselves, to our beauty and innocence, to our belief and our imagination that knows anything is possible. Because it *is*.

Anything is possible. You have to be still and listen, and you have to take the first step.

It is the hero's journey, returning home to oneself.

✎ Pivot

We all have defining, pivotal moments in our lives.

In those moments, a choice is presented and made, subconsciously or consciously. Often, the choice is covert, especially if you were a child. We are programmed with limiting beliefs and others' perceptions before we can even remember.

We internalize and react and choose based on our very limited knowledge and experience, based on subtext and unspoken messages around us.

One of my own pivotal experiences was the day we got the call that my father died. I was 11 years old. It was a Tuesday afternoon; my siblings and I had just gotten home from school. My best friend Mary was over, and we were playing cards with my sister. I heard the phone ring, and I felt it in my body: this was **not** good news. I got up and walked into the kitchen. Time stood still. As soon as my mother got off the phone, I saw her face. She didn't say a word, but I knew. After nine months of my father being in and out of hospitals and trying radical treatments for his rare form of lymphoma, his body had given in.

I walked slowly into the living room where we had been playing cards, and I said, "Mary, you have to go home now." She was speechless-she practically lived at our house-but she could see something big was going on. She left, and we gathered in the dining area near our kitchen.

That's what I remember. The intense grief as the reality, the finality, of death began to hit me, dropping me to the floor in heaving sobs.

I had a choice: to shut down my heart, or not. To feel (fully experience and process) my feelings, or not. But it didn't feel like a choice to me. It felt like survival. How could I possibly process the overwhelming grief that began coursing through me? Shutdown began.

My heart was frozen in time, in suspended animation, until I got the diagnosis that changed everything. Another pivotal moment. Because that's when I decided I didn't want to be closed off anymore. I've been unraveling that and walking home towards my heart, ever since. My heart was telling me (and likely had been for years) that it was time to wake up, that it was time to feel again, that it was time to get back to myself. My calling, my purpose. I had been hiding for too long. So here I am. Talking with you.

Now I can see that feeling and processing emotion is **always** the healthier, better choice. That's a lot of years of my heart being shut down, of living from a place of fear and disconnection.

♫ The Truth

I've always written songs. Music was my main form of communication, at least with the big feelings. The songs would express what I could not articulate in speech. They came through me, as opposed to from me, and my own healing would occur.

To this day, when I sit down at my piano to write or play through some of my songs, I feel much like Humpty Dumpty being put together again. Like all the lost pieces of me are returning home. And while I've written and journaled and composed for as long as I can remember, there's a greater purpose now. This is about aligning with my truth and sharing the light that is uniquely me. And in that way, giving others permission to be themselves, to follow their joy.

This is so much bigger than me. I can see that now, and it's a fire burning in me. There's no playing small anymore. There is feeling into the feelings–and telling my story as openly and honestly as I can. The doors open as I walk the path, and I have no idea where I'm headed. Except in the direction of my truth.

When we downplay and dismiss our voice, our desires, our unique passion and purpose, we do ourselves such a disservice. When we cease to imagine, when we snuff out that spark–that creative desire that we are dying to let ourselves express–we divert from our truth.

Transformation, internal evolution, change begins when we allow ourselves to dream, to imagine, to create, to see, to catch a glimpse, to perceive the glimmer that *there is more to me, to this life, this opportunity*. So often, we leave dreams behind for more predictable reality as we mature into adulthood.

Explore what's true for you. You will still be loved. You *are* enough. You *are* allowed. You *are* worthy. You get to have all that you desire for your life. So do I. And so does everyone. There is no lack; there is no competition; there are enough dreams and goodness and love to go around for everyone. In fact, as we listen and respond to our authentic longings, we create a ripple and open to the abundance already here, in this moment. We create ripples of positive, uplifting possibility for all when we give ourselves permission to be happy and fulfilled.

Trust. Allow. Believe.

✿ Origin Wounds

Everyone experiences trauma on some level. Those moments in time, those experiences, that felt scary. They were formative, and they made lasting impressions. In those moments, especially as children, we do what we think we need to do to survive. We shut down our hearts a little bit, to feel safe. We go inside ourselves and start protecting our hearts from a world that feels like too much to handle, from what feels like too much pain.

As children, often we don't understand how to manage or process our feelings, so we put ourselves in survival mode to cope with pain that feels like it will drown us. Our coping strategies, though they serve us for short-term survival, are not necessarily healthy for us long-term. It is in the unlearning and undoing of these childhood strategies, these limiting beliefs, that we will find our peace, our strength and our light.

❦ Fables

As young girls, we are told to be small, to stand down, to downplay our strengths and desires, to turn down our power. To young boys, we give equally damaging messages with a subtext of *don't have feelings* or at the very least *don't express them.* How damaging that is to put on our children, our child selves, our future! Giving ourselves and our children permission to feel and to be all that we are with no judgment . . . that is the greatest gift and act of kindness we can offer.

As I write, the sun is going down on a glorious autumn day. I begin to hear the cardinals chirp their goodnights to one another. The day winds down, and I am reminded how we get so many chances to live, so many opportunities to explore our dreams. The guidance is all around you and within you; the universe will never give up on you. Feel your passion and dreams, be joyful, revel in and express the beauty that is uniquely and undeniably you.

As night falls, I see the bats come out to play, swooping and diving, free and alive. This is their time, and they are embodying their joy. We all have the inherent right and ability to shine brightly and be joyful, and it's so important to give yourself permission to do so.

✤ Choosing

I was under the impression that I could not be both a writer/artist and a wife/mother. And these self-imposed limitations, this lack of vision and possibility, put me in the uncomfortable position of feeling as though I had to choose. This or that. You can't do both well. What a lie. What a narrow, linear way to approach such an amazing life.

And my lack of self-love and appreciation, my feelings of unworthiness, my failure to trust my inner voice caused me to turn my back on myself as a whole. I chose to be only part of my wholeness, while all along these various parts could have coexisted—and in fact, thrived. What caused me to think I couldn't have/be/do it all? Societal messages I'm sure, as well as familial cues or subtext.

The societal and familial circumstances were real, and the perceived messages felt real, but how that impacted and limited my life—that was all me. A disconnection from self and my higher power left me feeling angry, powerless and adrift. But as children, we don't usually know that we are choosing, that we are creating habits, pathways, and falsehoods that will inform our entire lives if we don't uproot them.

We must become aware of the weeds in the garden before we can pull them. We must go back and talk to that little child, to parent them in the most loving and kind way. You didn't know, then. You were so little. How could you have known that your experience of childhood would condition your perception and affect how you would see from that point forward? How could you have known that you held the key to your emotional freedom, that you held it in all these intervening years, if no one ever told you?

The thing is, you don't actually have to choose. You can have it all. You can be everything you want to be. You only have to be open to that, to know the possibility of that, and to step into your own life, to actively create what it is you see for yourself.

With no apologies. With utter confidence.

We do not need to subject ourselves to societal conventions and restraints, to confine ourselves to choosing only one path.

Life is not meant to be linear; it's meant to be expansive and 3-D and exponential.

✄ OBJECTIVE UNDERSTANDING

I was not expected in my family. I was deemed a surprise. My siblings would even tease me that I was adopted. My presence seemed to put a strain on my family in ways I couldn't understand or express. In response, I decided to be a rule follower, to be a people pleaser, to play small and stay invisible–especially so I didn't attract my father's wrath.

As much as I loved my father, his combustible temper would explode, seemingly unprovoked at times, without a moment's notice. It was terrifying for me as a small child, and the image of him physically punishing one of my brothers has stayed with me all of these years.

My eldest brother had the same potential for explosive, unbridled rage. During his teenage years and early 20s, out of all of our family, it most affected me, the empath. I lost hours of sleep at his rage and outbursts. From this vantage point, I can at least appreciate that he was expressing his emotions and not stuffing it down, as I did for so long.

I suppose no matter where you are in birth order, if there are several kids, you unwittingly compete for your parents' attention. It is a survival instinct that hasn't left our bodies. So I became a "good girl."

Please understand, all of this is not meant to elicit sympathy from you, the reader. I am in pursuit of my truth, on a personal archaeological dig, to unearth why I self-sabotage, why I don't believe in myself, my gifts and abilities, why I still hold myself back from greatness, why I still catch myself playing small, when I know better. Second-guessing and doubting myself and the importance of what I have to say, perhaps even in this moment, even as I write. One must unearth these ugly truths to look at them in the daylight to realize that they are small, they don't have control over us, and we can embrace them and tell them they don't have power over us anymore.

I felt unworthy for so long. So long that it felt like an intricate part of the fabric of my Being. I have not had the confidence to be who I truly am. Deep down. I have not spoken up or spoken out about the matters most important to me.

I am going there now. I am diving deep into my psyche and uprooting those early feelings of *I am not wanted, I am not important* and looking at them in the light of day for what they are: limiting beliefs. When we unearth these poisonous limiting roots of our own belief system, we can finally see them objectively, exposing them as lies that are internalized very young and that have no relevance to our true nature. Then we can let them wither away, leaving them to die, because these toxic thoughts cannot exist in the light, in our truth. They cannot control us any longer, once they are unearthed and looked at with love.

Shame keeps us bound to toxic thoughts, but love and clarity set us free of them. Standing in the real truth of who we are, shadow and light, enables us to accept ourselves as the perfect, work-in-progress humans that we are. And with compassion, we gain the strength to let go of the old stories and beliefs that do not serve our deep-down, important truths.

⟡ THE BELIEFS THAT HOLD US BACK

I remember going into my parents' bedroom one night a few months after my dad died. I woke my mom and told her that my heart had stopped. She was clearly frustrated, tired and dealing with her own grief. She told me to go back to bed. That if my heart "had actually stopped beating you wouldn't be able to *tell* me it stopped." It sounded reasonable. But I felt so alone in that moment. So very scared.

Looking back, I believe I was speaking about my energetic heart. I had tamped down my feelings and my fear to survive. And then I focused on what I thought I could control.

I took on everyone's hurt. I put others' needs before my own, repeatedly. It became my story. How I operated. If I could just be *good*, if I put others first, then people wouldn't leave me. I could control the outcome of the situation. And that paradigm of imagined safety that I created as a child shaped the next few decades of my life.

The communication in my family was mostly nonexistent. Definitely not healthy. Anger expressed in rage or suppressed in denial. Both of those, so stagnant. There can be no moving through pain, no healing, if no one acknowledges the pain. And there was so much unspoken, unprocessed pain.

Childhood. So many unvoiced, subtext, learned beliefs that impact the rest of our lives, if we are not vigilant. Sometimes it is like that. You are dealt a hand that was actually passed down from your parents, and theirs before them. I think it is key not to place blame for that. They were doing the best they knew how. As you are now. And you don't know what you don't know until you learn otherwise.

I ask you to imagine that your happiness, your purpose, your fulfillment *now*, in this moment in time, is your choice, and is within your power to transform. See, it's taken me half a lifetime to realize, to accept, that those choices were mine, that my actions were not forced upon me. Yes, I was trying to make sense of what I felt to be a very scary, chaotic world, but I *chose* those responses, those actions. I can see and accept that now.

Meditation:

The past is the past.
I let it go.
It serves me no longer.
I move forward.
This moment, this awareness.
I take it with me and forge a new path.
I get to create my own experience,
One positive, loving thought at a time.

✎ Parenting Yourself

So much is impressed upon us before the age of eight. So many unspoken roles are required of us. So many misinterpreted or misread cues.

We learned false messages when we were kids, and guess what? You get to release those beliefs. You know better now, and you get to parent yourself, love yourself and let go of all those old negative beliefs that no longer apply or serve you.

You are enough. You are worthy. You are whole.

Here's why it's important to go back, parent yourself and rescue that little kid:

When I was four years old, I watched my parents drive away, and I thought I would never see them again. My maternal grandparents came to stay with us–the four kids in my family–and though my parents were heading on a long-time-coming real honeymoon, I was certain that I had just become an orphan.

However I came into this world, this lifetime, perhaps needing to work through loss and letting go, the reality is that events we don't quite understand or know how to process between the ages of zero to seven can inform our internal mapping and our decision-making for the rest of our lives.

We must become aware of these recurring themes, recognize those patterns of choice for what they are, and go back and rescue that child, help them to understand that it was simply their perception at the time, a pathway, a groove in their mind that they can re-write and re-define.

I want to help that kid who thought cancer was contagious and struggled with going to see her father when he was dying, because she didn't want to catch it.

I want to hug that little girl and tell her that she can and must pursue her passion of songwriting–and that nothing should stop her from believing in herself, in her dreams.

I want to take her hand and let her know that it's okay to feel all the feelings, that she's not alone, that she's safe.

I can have that internal dialogue with my child self, and so can you. Time is not as linear as it seems, and we can re-parent from right where we stand.

✑ Then/Now

There is a little girl that wants to share her heart with the world.
There is a grown woman who understands now that she can, and
must, offer up the wisdom, music and light that she has been given.
The little girl was afraid to step out, to embrace her gifts, to own her
power. She thought she had to play small and be quiet to be deemed
valuable and to be safe. The grown woman understands that she is
and was and always will be valuable; she is enough, in all her beauty
and imperfections. She knows that she can embrace the whole of
her being, and she understands now that it serves no one for her to
hide her light.

The little girl's story (perception) was that one cannot be abundant
in their life's passion work; she thought that being successful at what
you love would fulfill your purpose and end your life early. That cost
was too high for her. The grown woman knows that there is no end
to her expansiveness, and that it is only by sharing her love and truth
with the world that she will be abundant, happy and free. She knows
that she can help set others free to be their best, most amazing, true
selves. She is charged with this responsibility and she accepts it. This
is her path, and she is excited as hell about it!

No one is served by keeping their gifts covered. We each carry beliefs,
perceptions, stories from long ago that limit us, that tamp down
our souls, that clip our wings. We must consciously make efforts to
unearth and rid ourselves of those. By unearthing those thoughts
and stories, bringing them into conscious analysis and investigation,
shining light on them, we see that they are not real. What IS real is
the power we have to create our lives and to imagine and then realize

in physical detail the full amazingness and splendor of who we are and what we bring to this conversation of Life.

If you get still and quiet, and can just Be, you will start to discern that muffled voice. You will know what lights you up, what path will bring you (and therefore others) the most *joy*. You will begin to know yourself, or more accurately remember yourself, your calling. You will begin to remember, and you will take a step to return home to yourself, your truth, your beauty. *Know thyself + unto thyself be true*

Even if you didn't understand it then, you can embrace it now: *You* are the gift. *You* are the light. *I AM the Gift. I AM The Love. I AM as God created me*

☙ Hiding My Light

If you had asked me twenty years ago, I would have said my favorite thing to do, and my joy to share, was playing piano and singing my original songs, to touch people through my music. That has not changed. What *has* changed is my openness about my gifts and who I am. My feelings of self-worth and value have dramatically increased since I began recognizing my soul and my light as something *worth* sharing and being.

In my early parenting years, there were people in my life who didn't even *know* I was a songwriter and musician. That's how deeply I had buried my identity. Music is, and always has been, the one thing to give me great joy, peace and comfort, and I was keeping it all to myself. A secret.

I was playing a house concert two years ago, and a man came up to me after the show. "Do you see that woman over there? That's my wife. And in 30 years, I've only seen her cry three times. Two of those times were tonight." I was so moved to hear that, to know the impact of the music, and I thanked him for sharing that with me.

Yes, sometimes people who listen to my songs cry. That's good. That is emotion moving, being processed. My music is emotional. It's heartfelt. It's true. It's universal. And it comes from something other than me.

Why do we hide our gifts? Why do we deny who we are and what we desire, our very essence? There is no real honor in that, though some of us are raised to believe that putting others first is where honor lies.

I am here to say that putting your *self* first, loving yourself, sharing your unique gifts: *That* is where the honor lies. Step boldly and proudly into your light, your gifts, your truth, your contribution to the world.

You are important. What you have to share is important. Your story is important.

Do not delay. Do not hide. Do not tamp down. Do not show up as less than the amazing, magnificent being of Light that you are meant to be.

☙ Being Seen

I remember vividly the first time I felt "seen." I was five years old, watching one of my favorite television shows on PBS. *Romper Room*. Each day, the host, the lead teacher, would take a few minutes at the beginning of the show to look into her "magic mirror" and say hello to some of the children who were watching. She would call out their names. In my mind, it was indeed complete and utter magic. Every day after my half-day kindergarten class, I ran downstairs to turn on the show.

And then it happened. She looked into her magic mirror and said, "I see Karen."

The feeling of joy, of being seen, validated, recognized ("we are here, we are here"!) swelled in me. It pulsed through my entire body. I ran through the house, "She said my name, she said my name!" My heart was bursting because, for the very first time, I felt like someone had finally seen me. I knew I was real, important, worthy of being seen and heard, of being called out on national television! That mirror really was magic.

I never had the chance to tell Miss Nancy of Romper Room how much that affected me, how much joy it brought me. And isn't it the case, so often, that the people whose words or actions impact us so profoundly don't even realize it?

You never know whose life you are changing with your words and actions.

❧ THE MAGIC OF CHILDREN

I learn from my children. I do. It is a mutual learning relationship. After all, there is a spiritual contract; they chose me for their mother for a reason, and I, in turn, learn so much about myself and about Life by walking this journey with them.

To be fair, it is much easier for me to love and appreciate their impact on my life when I am not in the day-to-day task of parenting. It is easier for me to contemplate the gifts they bring to my life as I sit in solitude, 700 miles away, at a writer's residency. But isn't that true of all relationships?

Getting some distance gives us perspective, hopefully some objectivity, about the very personal and subjective experiences that are human relationships. Including panning out on our relationship with ourselves. Clarity. We get these moments of clarity when we can stand back a bit. Like appreciating an abstract artist's work, looking at it from different angles.

The hope is that we're able to bring that earned clarity and stillness and knowing back with us, back from our pilgrimage to ourselves, our solitude, back to the relationships we hold dear.

I am reminded of Anne Morrow Lindbergh's "Gift from the Sea," where she writes:

When you love someone you do not love them, all the time, in the exact same way, from moment to moment. It is an impossibility. It is a lie to pretend to. And yet this is exactly what most of us demand. We have so little faith in the ebb and flow of life, of love, of relationships.

✑ Speaking Up

How long it has taken me to step into my power and magnificence, to cease playing small, to speak up, to speak out, to stand up, to shine brightly, to put aside others' opinions, to *be*. And yet, I suppose this is the perfect time for all of these pieces of my identity to re-emerge and re-assemble, to be in alignment. Because I believe in divine timing.

It so happens that I am an empath, a sensitive. For a long time, I used those gifts to be a people pleaser, both because I learned to do so in my childhood and because I have a strong desire to help others. But I am learning that living your life to please others does such a disservice to your calling, your individual purpose. You can be true to yourself and still help others in your own way.

Honoring our own light is what will, individually and collectively, create a huge, positive ripple outward and raise the vibration of all. It is something we must all take to heart: honoring ourselves, loving ourselves, and holding ourselves in high regard as the magnificent lights that we are. Pooling our collective consciousness, our uplifted awareness of self, is imperative for the well-being of all.

❧ And When the Rain Comes

When the rain comes, and inevitably it will, it helps us to slow down, to take stock, to listen. Every challenging situation is an opportunity, a golden opportunity to learn, to evolve, to expose our limiting beliefs and expel them from our consciousness. Instead of *Why me?*, an alternative such as *What can I learn from this?* is a beautiful way to start the conversation with yourself, your inner knowing, your higher power, however you name it.

The intuition you gain from asking that question–and then being in stillness and listening–is priceless. It is the beginning of the road map back to yourself, your truth and beautiful unique essence. There is no black and white, no 100 percent right or wrong. There is only being and choosing. And not choosing is still a choice.

Fear is the root cause of so many of the problems and suffering that we human beings endure. We must come from a place of curiosity, not judgment; from a place of love, not fear. Michael A. Singer calls this "witness consciousness" in his very enlightening book, "The Untethered Soul," which has been an invaluable guide for me.

We must look at our beliefs and our experiences from an observer's perspective, for healing and peace.

✎ Navigating in the Rain

I am in Martha's Vineyard.
I am riding a bike.
I am riding a bike in the rain.
For the adventure of it.

I am on my bike, in the rain, on my way to a coffee shop. It feels like it's taking me forever, and the rain is getting harder and harder. My coat, my jeans, everything is soaked through.

"Why is my GPS steering me wrong?" I wonder aloud. "It said a 14-minute ride . . . this must be twice that now."

Um, helloooo?!! Maybe I didn't *hear* the GPS because it was at the bottom of my bag. Ohhhhhh.

I am beginning to see. You have directions, or think you do. You start moving, and you miss the pivotal moment, the detour, and you're circling and circling in the rain. You can't see where you're going, and you can't hear any guidance.

This is what it's like when we go it alone, when we unplug from our internal knowing, our unique mapping system. We have a purpose to fulfill, and if there is too much interference, we can't do that. We need to be able to listen, to turn when necessary, to access that map we carry inside of us. Especially when a storm is brewing.

Isn't it uncanny how, after you arrive at your destination, with all the twists and turns, all the detours and side trips, all the winding roads and squinting through the rain for the road signs, the trip back home always feels so short?

How did it take me so long to get here? I wonder. *I was just around the corner* (metaphorically and literally), AND

Thank goodness I didn't turn around and head home without the adventure. Just because of a little rain.

Into every life, the rain must fall. And the rain is good. Don't be afraid of the rain. Don't wait to live your truth because you fear the rain may dampen things. Just do it. Trying is the only option. The outcome is less relevant. Stay connected, and imagine the possibility.

Interestingly, the rain stopped once I let go of my expectations of timing, embraced the uncharted adventure of it all, and just started looking around and enjoying what is: the changing leaves, blown around by the wind and the rain.

I hear the cardinal chirp and I keep pedaling.

☙ SERENDIPITY

I picked up the phone and dialed the number that was listed on the website. I guess in this age of remote connection, texting, and emails, I didn't actually expect a human being to answer.

But answer, she did. "Hello?"

Ummmm. Awkward pause. "Nancy?" I asked. "Yes, this is Nancy."

To myself: *Oh. Wow . . . okay.*

To Nancy (streaming words together faster than I normally do): "Well. Hi. I'm not really sure WHY I'm calling, except I've been reading your book and I'm here on the island and I thought 'I need to speak with this person' (she was so real and funny and accessible in her book) and then I saw this number and so I dialed. Funny, huh?"

I am following the little voice. I am listening. I did not for so many years. I hung up on it. I tuned it out. I stuffed it down. But up here, in the solitude of autumn on this beautiful island, I can hear so clearly.

"I just found out about you and your book *Writing from the Heart* a month ago," I heard myself saying. "I've not been able to put it down, and I really felt inspired to call you and meet. Or at least talk." Words kept coming out of my mouth, of their own volition. "As a matter of fact," I said, "I don't usually do this sort of thing, but I'm listening to my intuition now, and it's gotten so loud and relentless"!

Then Nancy told me a little story about how she, too, had called another author that she respected, in *her* early writing days: Anne

LaMott. I chuckled and said, "Nancy, the only other book I brought up here besides yours is 'Bird by Bird' by Anne LaMott." She replied "I bet the Universe is having a good chuckle over this!" I absolutely agree.

Amazing where you will be led if you stop and listen, and then act. I am being guided.

I'm still pinching myself. Did I really just make that call, and did Nancy Aronie really just answer? Could the mentors be right here for me, that easily?

Heck, yeah! That easily.

(We are the ones who get in the way and make it difficult.)

✹ REUNITED

I am so grateful to be connected with my higher power again. I feel relaxed, joyful, all is well. I am not alone, and every need I have is met as I continue on my path of healing and shining my unique light. Anyone who encounters my story or my music will be touched by Love, and my hope is that it will give them the courage to look at their own story and heal, learn from it, and begin to create their story now, in their own way.

The idea of co-creating our lives is so powerful, so life-changing. Add to that the mindset that abundance is and always has been here for us, that we are provided for in the deepest sense, and this is life-altering.

My friend Tara said to me once, "You *are* the church." I love this. I finally get what she meant now. I can bring people together in love, healing, music and story; to promote wellness, individual and collective; to share the Divine Love that is available to us all.

In truth, we are *each* and *all* the church, and when we come home to ourselves, we can see that so clearly.

❧ Showing Up for Yourself

Being a warrior, a hero in your life, means acknowledging where you are now–and understanding that the path forward starts with one step and a healthy dose of trust. When we take emotional risks and are guided by our intuition, we are aligning with our truth, our essence. It is not always the easy path, but it is always the best path. Be kind and loving with yourself, with where you are right now. Accept, open, allow, trust. Your inner being knows who you are and what you want to be and express. Trust the voice, the inner knowing, and take the next right step or action.

✲ Being Kind to Ourselves

We are *all* good enough. What we say, do, who we are. It's more than enough.

Diving deep doesn't have to be sad or painful or difficult. It can be a joy-filled positive experience unfolding. Let's untell the stories that we've used for so long to justify our pain. Let's rebuild our lives how we want to see and experience them. We can choose to stay stuck, or we can choose our truth. Our essence. Our joyful being.

We get to decide, to choose what we want for our lives. We decide how we will respond–victim or survivor. Every challenge and obstacle is an opportunity, a re-direction. We can listen in the stillness, and take action from that place of stillness, instead of imposing our will on it. Divine guidance has everything we need, and it provides for us in ways we can scarcely imagine for ourselves.

It's so important not to give pieces of your divine self away. At all times, stand guard at the door of your soul, and honor your purpose, your highest joy.

This is the kindest act you can bestow upon yourself, and indeed, on all of us.

🐚 LOVE OVER FEAR

Fear: It's a powerful emotion, a reaction. It can stop you in your tracks, freeze you to your core. Fear is often the emotion that compounds whatever origin wound we are holding in our hearts. It gets stuck, and then we keep trying to cover it and bury it so that we don't have to feel the wound. But that does not get rid of it. It only serves to bury our heart, our light, deeper and deeper, and that causes more pain than the original wound. Untreated and unprocessed, it will only wreak more havoc in our lives.

Our most beautiful state is the state of love. When we allow (or in childhood it happens unconsciously) fear to take over, we disconnect from a sense of love and well-being, and we think we are on our own to face the world and its harsh realities. Our natural state is one of love, joy and peace–and we are never alone. But directly or indirectly, choosing fear over love causes pain and suffering far greater than your origin wound. If we can tap into the wound and the fear, and let it move through us, if we can sit with and process the pain, then we are free from that pain. It no longer holds any power over us. We are washed clean; we are freed; we can stand in love.

We all have a point in time that we may recall–or perhaps were too young to recall– a disconnect point. The fall from grace. For me, it was the phone call that my father had died. It was an emotional crossroads. One path was to feel the pain; the other was to numb the pain, turn it off, start "doing" and keep busy to avoid the reality and depth of the pain. And that is exactly what I did.

The grief, from my 11-year-old perspective, would do me in. I was suspended in fear. It was too much to bear, to feel, and I thought I'd never recover. I could feel the importance of this moment in my life as it was transpiring, even at such a young age.

People can spend entire lifetimes wrapping their hearts and avoiding that origin pain, but going back in there and opening our hearts and processing that pain (which often isn't as big or scary as we've made it out to be) is a doable, efficient path back to Love, to our truth, to our simple beauty and perfection. It's never too late to learn to shed the layers that numb our hearts and to feel true joy again.

Human existence can be challenging, even painful, at times. Since we are souls, beings of light having a human experience in this body, we can transcend what comes at us in the physical form. Every challenge is an opportunity for growth, a choice you make to learn from and evolve.

I am not diminishing anyone's pain or trauma. I am suggesting that how we approach the challenge, how we react or respond, makes all the difference. How we see it is up to us. There are lessons always, and I daresay that one can find a silver lining amidst even dire circumstances.

Fear fuels pain and suffering. It makes us close off our hearts. It creates illness. It stifles relationships. Fear comes from a scarcity mindset ("there's not enough to go around"), and we often respond to fear by attempting to exert control in various areas in our lives.

Ring any bells? "If I can just do *this thing*, control *this outcome*, then _____ won't come to pass".

In fact, fear creates a swell of energy around the very thing that you fear, and that energy becomes attracted to you. The very thing you fear, when given attention, fuels the negative energy and makes the circumstance more difficult.

Love is the opposite of fear. Love dissolves fear, as the two cannot coexist in the same space, thought, moment. Choosing a response of Love gives fear the heave-ho. When we are in alignment with our highest selves, there is only love, only light, only truth.

Every human being has the power to quiet the ego and get out of the way so that abundance and creativity can do their thing. Get on the yoga mat, or say a silent prayer, or sit in meditation for a bit. When we stop doing and controlling, we stop running from our truth and we can BE, we can sit and listen and heal and know our truth in a deeply profound and unique way.

Most of us are born with a healthy sense of risk aversiveness that's been wired into humans for years to keep our species safe and alive. But when being safe begins to perpetuate a sense of fear, when the scales tip in the direction of fear, that certainly holds us back. Fear is limiting and debilitating, and it keeps us from realizing our gifts and being our best, highest selves. I will not let fear stop me anymore. Fear does not get a say in my reality, in my co-creation.

Thought:

I open up to the light of day
Fear no longer in my view
I can do what I came here to do:
To help you see your love, your light, your grace
To learn to embrace the shadow and light,
The pieces that make you whole.

PART TWO

𓆰 Using Your Voice

There are many ways to use your voice for healing and transformation.

The first (and perhaps most obvious and simple) is to physically speak your truth: set boundaries, verbally state what it is you want for your life with confidence, say daily empowering affirmations out loud.

A second way is to use your voice to make simple sounds on your exhale breath: sound like the wind, or a snake; sound like a child squealing with delight; sound like a fire engine siren. Just play with sound, with your voice, to get in touch with your primal voice.

A third way that I have found very valuable is to do some toning on different notes, to stir up and clear out from your energetic body any negativity or resistance to your growth and evolution. I love to teach this in my workshops, because every attendee feels so much more grounded and open after the experience of chakra toning.

These are some simple ways to get in touch with your physical voice and your deep truth so that you can be empowered to move forward and to claim your ideal life.

✑ Don't Sweat the Small Stuff

Thought:

It comes and goes. Life ebbs and flows.
The only thing permanent is change.
We must let go, let things flow,
Holding on tightly brings pain.

Zoom out. Being too close, looking too hard, is the ego's distraction; it's a form of procrastination, and it undermines your focus, your passion, your happiness. We all have something we need to share. Follow your joy, and share it with the world. Don't listen to your inner critic. Be still, and listen to your inner *knowing*.

You mustn't let society or anyone else dictate who or what to be. You are the master of your thoughts and the creator of your reality. You are responsible for your own happiness. Period.

Zoom out. The day-to-day events don't matter so much. The way in which we move through our day and relate to others, that *does* matter. If we could see around the details, the minutiae, rise above, we would understand that we are not a body with a soul, but a soul having a human experience.

Silence distills divine essence. It is in the quiet solitude that we begin to truly open, to remember the Divine that is within, and we begin to get glimpses of how to return to ourselves, in wholeness and love.

It took one major mind-blowing incident to unravel the tapestry of fear and denial and unworthiness that I had spent years weaving around my heart.

Thoughts of *I'm not good enough* or *My voice doesn't matter* (does that sound familiar?) melted away as I realized that fear had been running the show, and I was no longer willing to allow that to happen. Love, Truth and Joy became my executive producers. I was faced with a diagnosis to shake me out of my complacency, my cocoon of fear, helplessness and denial. It launched me to action, to finally embrace my voice, my message, and step into my desire to share my wisdom and light with the world.

No longer holding back, no longer shameful or less than, choosing to embody the amazing unique goodness that I am. (That we all are.) I have a purpose. You have a purpose. You can feel the tug of your heart. You can hear the whisper in your ear despite all of the noise of the small stuff . . . I *know* you can.

Zoom out.

✑ Forgiveness and Love

Forgiveness and love. Forgiveness and love. Forgiveness and Love. They go hand in hand. You must forgive yourself (and others) before true love can come through. The deepest sort of love. Self-love.

With forgiveness, you can open your heart. Allow your heart to soften. Allow your heart to lead you. Trust your heart. Trust your path. Love will light the way.

Witnessing objectively and without reaction is a tool, a route to love and forgiveness. *And also . . .* you get to set healthy boundaries that serve to keep you well and happy and on purpose. Sharing your light is the whole point of this (or any!) lifetime. And if someone doesn't see, understand or get your Light, your divine essence, that is not your concern.

You cannot change others. You cannot *make* them see the light. You are responsible only for your own light, nurturing that, keeping it aflame. When you pay attention to that, and to the desires that lead you to the next right step, you will be truly listening. You will feel fulfilled. You will be accessing your joy, your best and highest self. You can only know your own path, and what is right and true for you, in this moment.

Open your heart, see what you uncover.
–From my song, Love is Waiting

✿ REDEMPTION

Your story is one of healing, of being lost, then finding your way, finding redemption. That is the journey we are all on. Each one will look different, but the arc is the same. There are lessons along the way, sometimes difficult, that help us access our Truth, that enable us to share our story and our light in a more profound way. We each have things we are here to learn in this lifetime, in order to create a ripple of impact in a positive, loving way.

Regardless of your medium, your background, your education, your race, color or creed, you have something unique to share. And it is in the sharing that healing and transformation can occur. For you, and for those whose lives and hearts you touch. It starts with one small step in the direction of love. That's all you need.

You can *do* this. The world needs your gifts, the light that uniquely shines forth from you. This is an enormous tapestry, no two squares alike, and how glorious, beautiful, magnificent it is! Let us *all* enjoy your beautiful colors and textures. <3

✿ RELATIONSHIP

The most important relationship we have is with ourselves. If we can love, care for, nurture ourselves, there's no limit to what we can do and be!

We are each enough.
In and of ourselves.
Complete.

I believe that the biggest thing that enhances our relationship with ourselves is understanding our connection to the universe, of our energetic nature, that we are part of the whole–we are the stuff that stars are made of.

With this understanding, we get a sense of our magnitude, our importance, our connection to Source, to all of Life, to Love. Then we can deeply and completely love ourselves for the magic that we are.

S Who Are You?

It may help to think about what makes you *you*. Or even to think about who or what you are *not*, to get to your truth.

What are some amazing things about you that you are so proud of, that you feel good about? What are the limiting messages you have received or have taken on in your lifetime? These can be unlearned and replaced with empowering positive messages. Repetition of positive messages creates energy around them, and habits can be changed!

If someone asked you to name the one thing that you most want to accomplish or be in this lifetime, what would you respond? No judges, no censors, no editors.

Sometimes it feels easier to ride the waves of external life that carry us, that propel us. To operate on auto-pilot since maybe it's working "well enough." Taking responsibility for our own happiness requires effort and thoughtful action and patience. We must turn inward and remember . . . remember the joy and creativity that filled our days before we "grew up" and became adults. We have the freedom to reconnect to our joy and to share that magic with the world. When we know who we are, our joy ripples outward and actually changes the collective energy. When we know who we are, the collective consciousness of humanity is raised.

✑ Subjective Reality

My dad. He was loved by everyone. He was charismatic, talented, witty, a successful entrepreneur; there wasn't a person in the town where I grew up who didn't know and love my father. Of course, he was my personal idol as well. He was like magic to my child-mind. He was everything I'd hoped to be as a grown up: happy, successful, talented, a friend to all he met, doing what he loved for a profession. He would sneak pop songs into the church service by playing them super slowly or in a minor key so that the priest wouldn't catch on. He had a great laugh.

For so long, I only remembered those things.

But my dad wasn't perfect. And losing him when I was 11 didn't really give me the opportunity to see that in real time. To see his flaws. The imperfections. The shadow side that we all have. By the time he got sick and died, I was still in "my father is amazing" mode. I didn't get to the rebellious teenage years with him around, to realize that he actually "didn't know anything" as kids often do at that developmental stage. And it took me so long to internalize the reality of my father. My full experience of my father. The whole 360 degrees: that he yelled sometimes, and it frightened me; that he got frustrated and angry easily; that he may not have been as fulfilled as I thought he was. Surely he had emotional baggage himself from losing his own father when he was in college.

My point is this: we idealize our memories. We can have a certain perspective or recall that isn't shared by others (even in the same family) of the exact same circumstances.

Our realities are subjective. Why not use that to our benefit? Imagine the perfect reality for your own life, and then create it.

Visualize what you want for your life, and then go to town taking action steps to make it your reality.

Because our reality? Our experience? It begins in our subconscious mind.

๑ GIFTS AND GROWTH

We are given gifts all the time. Moments, glimpses, circumstances that help us grow and help us increase our gratitude, if we let them. If we notice. If we are aware.

What are we to learn? What are we to understand? What are we to change? To be? To do?

In his podcast episode with Gabrielle Bernstein, Russell Brand says, "We are more reptilian than mammal because we shed our old skin and become anew so very often." That is, if we let ourselves grow and evolve. If we don't force ourselves to stagnate. Growth and change is our natural state.

If we are not growing, we are dying in some way, great or small. If we are resisting or stagnating, we are working against our natural rhythm and our organic nature. You do not observe a tree, come springtime, say "No, I will not allow those buds to grow this year. I am tired. I am just not in the mood." Nature and natural processes will take over, and nature will always prevail.

We do ourselves and others such a disservice to dig our heels in and refuse to grow and change. Sometimes this refusal comes from fear, but sometimes it stems from just not knowing, not having the awareness. Maybe your truth and your light got tamped down as you tried to make sense of our world, your family, your experience and felt it safer to withdraw and stay small. Maybe you were taught to stay in line and not take risks, that safer is better.

Let us honor the natural divinity within us, let us grow our light and shine brightly, as is our inherent, amazing nature. We are meant to fully step into and embody our power and our Being. Resisting growth only causes pain and suffering. Live your truth, be all that you are, and continue to expand.

✑ THE OPENING

It has been a real process, opening my heart again.

Truly opening my heart.
Listening to my heart.
Following my heart.

I didn't realize how shutting it down, ignoring it over and over–what a massive job that did on my heart, how it informed my life and my experiences, all the pain it caused.

My diagnosis was clearly the wakeup call I needed. I was not hearing and seeing all of the other signs and messages.

Looking back, I recall so many opportunities, but I kept protecting my heart instead of growing and expanding.

I sometimes picture how frustrating that was for the Universe, for my spirit guides and guardian angels. I'm so grateful they didn't give up on me. I feel so grateful to have landed here, open-hearted and filled with purpose.

✶ SUPERPOWERS

All of my songs have been gifts through the years, messages of love, guiding me back to my heart. And I thought I was only writing them for other people! As I go back and play through songs, I am always amazed at how the message could be for me, or for anyone. How personal yet universal these messages are. That's how I know that these songs are important; they are a big part of my mission, of my work and my purpose.

Tanya Carroll Richardson refers to empaths who feel a call to help people deeply as "earth angels" in her book *Are You an Earth Angel?* I've known deep in my bones for a long time that I am: I'm meant to help others, to make a difference on their journey, by saying or singing what is comforting or inspiring. I've always known my songs to be healing, but I wasn't quite sure how to reach people, or if they would listen. I didn't believe that what I had to say could be inspiring or important to others. I didn't believe in my own voice, in the uniqueness of my music and my message.

I've learned those physical details are not my concern. Now I trust in a divine path, in synchronicity. If I write it, whoever needs to hear these messages, these words, will find them, will hear them. I know now that there are people, an audience in the truest sense, that are ready to hear the messages of these songs, and it is my work to put these out into the world.

Music is my power tool, my catalyst to healing. Connection through songwriting is my superpower! What is *your* superpower? What do you feel called to do, what lights you up, what are you so passionate and aligned with, that you *must* share it with the world?

☙ Hard Things Via Puppies

I have learned some important lessons recently. They weren't easy either. I have learned: I can commit to something and not quit. I can do hard things. I can continue to open my heart to Love, and it will make my life even more amazing.

It's the lens we look through that shapes our experience. I had been looking through a lens of lack, negativity and fear. It was making everything in my life seem hard and unmanageable. Especially adopting a puppy.

My daughter had found him on Craig's List and we went and picked him up. And then I (very quickly) wanted to give him away. It was like having a newborn again, and I was not prepared for that. I regretted saying yes to this family addition. He was a great comfort and distraction for my kids during the pandemic quarantine period in late 2020, but I had forgotten how much work a puppy was.

We were in the kitchen with this tiny dog, and I hadn't been sleeping well. Housetraining takes great dedication, and I was tired. Really tired. I told my kids that we would have to let him go, that our friends were going to take him into their family. It was a heart-wrenching conversation, and I felt like the worst mother in the world.

So we drove the puppy to our friend's house, all the while a nagging feeling in my gut, like something was off. Like I knew deep down I wasn't giving myself a real chance here.

I ended up driving around for hours in distress, only to go back to our friend's home and ask for the puppy back. I hurt them in the process, and I hurt my kids.

But through this experience, my daughter reminded me that I am strong and I am loved, that I didn't have to quit on her, my son, or the puppy, that I didn't have to quit on myself.

Adding more love and commitment in areas of my life doesn't take away from my work, my writing, my healing. In fact, it's an important part of my evolution. Love in any form will always enhance my work.

And I am learning, living, loving like never before. I am engaging in the messiness of real relationships and commitments. I am being imperfect, and knowing I am still loved. This was not a message I understood in my own childhood, and yet my child has taught me this. I am grateful for her loving heart and her integrity as a person.

My knee-jerk reaction to the change and responsibility of a puppy was to shut down my heart, *again*. It's always my go-to, protective response. I am working to recognize this and to keep my heart open, to fully experience all of life and love. I am so incredibly blessed and also I know I'm always learning. This was a hard lesson: letting this puppy go and then realizing, *I don't want to shut down my heart*.

I choose love over fear. I choose *love*.

✺ Integrity

I am not proud of my recent behavior. I did not act with integrity. I was reactive and operating from a place of fear. I didn't honor my commitment and I didn't honor a promise.

Despite all of this, I have discovered–uncovered perhaps–that I *am* worthy. I am worthy of abundance and joy, I am worthy of love and prosperity, I am worthy despite, and even because of, my flaws, my humanness.

If I can love myself after this experience, after the way I reacted and was spinning ferociously, if I can come out the other side of this with valuable information about who I am, my aspects of light and dark, and I can love myself through all of this, then I am *onto* something. Some true and deep healing.

Uncovering that, from a very young age, I didn't feel worthy to enjoy unconditional love, I didn't feel worthy of having this joy, I didn't feel prepared or enough–that is a giant step toward healing that old wound.

Acknowledging and feeling *into* it, airing it out, is the only way to move through something and heal. Of course it's best to do this in the moment, but I forgive myself these imperfections. I love myself despite my fear, my feeling unworthy. I love myself back into wholeness. Into joy. Into who I am meant to be, who I always was, my whole and beautiful truth.

I remember thinking that I wasn't sure if I had enough stories, real transformative, inspiring stories and wisdom to share as I embarked on this book. Well, I added to my repertoire when this puppy entered my life, and this wisdom was not gained without some painful growth, some letting go, some painful consequences to my loved ones.

I will remember and speak of this, to talk about feelings of unworthiness that so many of us carry with us, like a heavy weight. I will talk about forgiveness and love for myself, the importance of seeing my whole self, of loving all of me.

I am a work in progress.

✤ BREATHE

I remember standing at my desk at Duke University, performing the administrative job I had held for seven years, and thinking, *I am not breathing*. Literally. I had exhaled and what might have been an eternity passed before I realized I had not inhaled.

How long had it been since I had taken a deep breath? I felt so much pressure and anxiety to perform well at my job and in my life as a mother and wife that I had not even noticed my inability to fill my body with air, as the clock ticked.

My body was trying to tell me something. I was giving and giving in so many areas of my life and was not good at receiving, at listening to what I really wanted and needed. Including taking a minute to just breathe. Inhale. Receive air.

When we stop listening, when we walk away from our calling, when we bury our truth, we stop the flow of the positive and creative life force. If we turn away from ourselves, our truth, it serves no one, least of all us. There is no peace or joy there because there is no light allowed in.

Once we recognize that we have chosen (consciously or not) to be frozen in our hearts, we can start the process of freeing ourselves. In the quiet moments, the stillness, the spaces when we notice we have not inhaled in far too long, we can listen, and we can get a glimpse of the magnificence of our unique light. Then, we can step into or toward that light. We can return home to ourselves, our truth, to the oneness that we are.

I like the idea that we are not bodies with a soul, we are souls having a human experience. We hold onto sadness and heartache, we protect ourselves and stay small, we constrict, because it feels safe there. But the place we are truly safe is a place of alignment, within ourselves and with a source of Love that is greater than us.

We are all One, all part of the great Love, the Big Love, and we are here to learn, grow and evolve. If we are not growing, we are dying. We're forgetting to breathe.

So be still and listen. Return to your *home*. Your breath will guide the way.

⟡ Creating Your Life

There are many stories in our lives that we recall from our past that are perspective, not reality; the experience of our experiences, if you will. Once you let all of that go and imagine a blank canvas, you can create your life in the full glory you wish it to be.

You are the co-creator of your life, in concert with Source energy, but it means you have to go off-script, you have to go rogue from what the ego has you believing, away from how the ego limits you to play it safe.

When you get a glimpse of a beautiful, public garden in full bloom in springtime, it's a wonder to behold. I think it is like that when we first understand how we are, very much, co-creating our lives every day, in every moment, and with every choice, thought and word.

It's like being a kid in a huge candy shop:

They have these? These are my favorites!

Wait, I can have an entire bag of those?

Oh man, I haven't seen this kind in years!

All of it. Available to you. In every moment. Every big beautiful vision that you have for your life.

Obviously, we can't smell every flower at the same time, or fit all the Red Hots into our mouths at once.

But it's all there, ready and waiting for us: whenever we decide that we are worthy and we know what we want.

Sometimes I feel like Rip van Winkle, waking after being asleep for *so* many years of my life. I'm awake! I'm participating in my own life experience.

🔥 Visualization

Our minds are tricky. Very clever. When our ego runs the show, so often it is replaying old stories, old beliefs that served us as children and no longer do. We keep ourselves safe, but this blocks us from truly expressing our deepest essence. It takes awareness and commitment to change these patterns, these beliefs engrained in neuro-pathways and playing on repeat.

We need to be aware of their existence, know that they once held purpose for us, and kindly thank them and let them go. And it is *key* to replace them with new, positive, growth-mindset neuro-pathways. If we do not *replace* them, these messages and beliefs will creep back in. The mind is clever that way.

We can choose to challenge our limiting beliefs and create a new belief system, one with no ceiling, no walls–anything you desire for your life, you can create. Daily practice of the awareness, and then committing to replacing the old patterns with new thriving ones, is so important.

There is enough joy, abundance, love for everyone. But we must step into the light of possibility, and out of the realm of fear-based consciousness.

Gratitude is a wonderful tool for elevating your consciousness. When we focus on the aspects of our current experience that we are grateful for, it primes the pump for more goodness and abundance in our lives.

We must see what we desire in our mind's eye. We must visualize and fully embrace it daily.

And then, we let go.

Do things that bring you joy, and allow the universe to reorganize energy in alignment with your highest intention and desires. We must surrender control and trust that these aspects of our physical experience are on our way to us.

Trust, allow, believe, receive.

⚘ Questioning and Resistance

I imagine we all have moments of questioning, of resistance to taking a leap of faith and following our hearts. Uncertainty takes over, and resistance kicks in. It's easier and safer to turn a deaf ear because maybe on some level we don't believe we are worthy or good enough to create that art, that book, that nonprofit organization, that invention, that offering.

I resisted. I knew that this gift of music was a magical one, that it held great powers of transformation and healing within it. I *knew*, on some level, but I still let fear and beliefs of unworthiness rule my course.

I stopped listening.

I stopped trusting.

What *really* happened, I believe, was that I unplugged. I disconnected from any form of higher power, and then my screen went blank.

All I had to do was say "yes" to find that connection again. But it took many years, and a diagnosis, before I would. It is okay to ruminate and question. When you sit in stillness and listen, and you know in your heart you have something to share and then, consciously or unconsciously, still don't share your gifts or your truth, you do such a disservice to yourself and to all of humanity.

The soul that is uniquely *you*, you have something to offer. Deep down you know that, and you have always known that. But we disconnect. We get scared. We get overwhelmed, maybe. We feel unsure.

It does not have to be hard. We do not have to fight it. Our truth, our gifts, they are there for a reason. Let's unearth all that. Let's heal ourselves. Let's reconnect. Let's live what's real, and find what's true for each of us.

Basking in the sunlight,
Or bathing in the moon
Hold on to what is true.
–From my song, True

⟡ Cut the Cord

The best response you can have to any negative or dark behavior of people around you is to bring more light, more love. And be mindful not to dip into that low-frequency vibration they are giving off. Keep your vibration high and don't let others' negativity and energy and fear drain your energy or attach to you. Cut the cord.

Each morning, I affirm to keep my vibration high no matter what comes my way, to spread love and light all while protecting my energy and setting healthy boundaries.

It's healthy to set boundaries on your time, your energy, your relationships. You can choose what you want to do, with whom, when and for how long. You do not have to fix everyone else's life or challenges. You do not have to run yourself into the ground to prove that you are worthy.

You are already worthy of your own love, attention and care. If there's a relationship or situation that does not feel good, or makes you uncomfortable, have a conversation about it. But know in advance what you are willing, or not willing, to do in terms of your own well-being. Put yourself first. The focus for you is *you*.

Living consciously and with love, for yourself and others, makes a profound impact on you and everyone you come in contact with.

✿ NATURE

Have you looked around recently? Step outside, and have a look. Look around. Look *up*. It is magnificent, yes? So much beauty in our natural world for us to enjoy. The chirp of the cardinals in the trees, the trees themselves, flowers, sky, clouds, rainbows, all of it–it's so dang inspiring! So many gifts Mother Nature offers us. Don't rush by them.

Stop. Breathe. Take it all in.

The simplicity and the complexity of it all. Natural elements have always seeped into song lyrics and poetry - nature is so profound and inspiring - and most definitely universal.

The natural world offers us wisdom and guidance. Nature can be our personal guide to inner knowing and wisdom. Nature holds our truth. Nature is Source Energy made manifest for us to access the beauty and joy of this life. There are different entry points: nature, music, meditation, stillness, yoga; you choose what resonates for you.

✿ The Big Love

All I feel these days is *love*. Love for strangers, love for those who push my buttons, love for my children and ex-husband, love for myself, love for the human experience, love for the challenges and opportunities. It's as if I've jumped into a large, warm pool of love, and I never want to step out. It's warm here, and peaceful. It makes everything better.

Everyone I meet will feel this massive, warm love, and they will know the light pouring out of me is truth.

There is nothing but *love*. Love is the only thing that is real.

✆ So Much Goodness

I cannot tell you how many times I've written a song and then thought, *Oh wow, this person should hear this message. It's definitely meant for them . . . -*-only to realize that it's also meant for me, and in turn, for all. Because these songs are universal, and we can all relate to the emotions and thoughts contained within them. Phew. I am so glad that the Universe does not give up on us.

It sure did take a lot of knocking, for many years, for me to finally realize that the knocking was for me, that I had to turn the knob and open the door. And then when the door was opened? I had to walk *through* it. No one else could do it for me, and no one else can do it for you either.

It takes courage. Vulnerability. Trust. Listening to your gut. Loving yourself enough.

Whatever messages we thought we heard, whatever self-doubt and shame we internalized, we must rewrite the script. We must free ourselves.

I have been given this amazing gift, to be able to turn feelings into powerful songs. Who am I to *not* do that? Who am I to just ignore the gift, to walk away? Songs are important; if you let them, they can crack you open and heal you all at the same time. Let the light come in through the cracks.

Trust is a big part of the creative process. Trust yourself and your intuition. And trust that Creativity will not let you down. It will come through you as you open up. It always does. And the co-creation will be magical. I guarantee that.

❧ Possibility

We are here to learn, grow, unlearn, and remember.

The journey home is about listening and reclaiming the unique truth that is yours, a truth that is enough and worthy and desires to be expressed through you in this world.

Life can be busy and distracting, and we owe it to ourselves to set aside time every day, even 15 minutes, to sit and be with our thoughts, to let the dust settle so that we can see what is there, to let our truth become clear.

When we observe and notice, we automatically begin to shift. Doors open, ideas come, change can transpire. New messages begin to drown out the old ones; we can, little by little, replace limiting beliefs with phrases of empowerment and optimism, like:

I am worthy.
I am enough.
My path and heart are important.
What I have to offer will help the world.
My truth is important.
My joy is my birthright.
I choose to love myself.
I choose to live from a place of love.

Being the hero of your own life means empowering yourself to take action, to create the life that you want to be living, to create your happiness. No one else can do this for you or me. It is your responsibility. And the sooner you claim your responsibility for your happiness, the sooner you will remember who you are and what your purpose is.

Thought:

It is so easy to remove ourselves from the responsibility of listening. There are so many diversions, tasks to do, calls to make, so much noise and clutter that gets in our way of sitting in silence, listening and being. We have to commit to creating space for the intuition, inspiration, and divine nudges that our inner self really wants us to hear and know. To dream is to let yourself be still and open to possibility.

PART THREE

✑ Commitment

Life is precious. Fragile. Amazing. An adventure. A gift.

We have an opportunity, *in every moment*, to choose. To say *yes* to the expansive new thought, to allow ourselves to grow, to open, to be aware. Self-awareness is a daily choice. A commitment to uncovering, remembering, celebrating who you are, who you were born to be, the gifts that you came here to share, the learning you came here to do.

This is the Big Love I speak of. The all-encompassing, forgiving, compassionate warmth that you feel when you stand in the Light, in your Truth. When you give yourself time to sit in the silence and stillness, and just be and feel. You *know* who you are. You've always known.

But we sometimes forget as life happens.

I do believe that we cannot create change in our lives if we keep doing the same actions. Over and over. Or keep having the same thoughts. Again and again. We must love and accept ourselves in this moment, and be at peace with where we are, while also visualizing and creating what changes and conditions we desire in our lives.

We must combine intention with guided intuitive action.

✿ CRACK OF LIGHT

Anne Lamott writes in "Bird By Bird":

This shaft of light, sometimes only a glimmer, both defines and thwarts the darkness.

To me, this means that we just need a small glimpse of light, a crack, a pinhole even, to be able to discern the difference between light and dark–to become aware that the darkness does exist. I think this leads us naturally to understand that we are all light and dark, that a balance of the two is necessary. Without embracing our shadow-self, we cannot fully embrace our whole self, which is utterly important and necessary for true self-love.

Comfort is convenience; maybe even laziness. It's definitely an easier path, to numb out and not take responsibility for your life, your choices, your circumstances. It's much easier to blame others and your past. But where are you right now, in this moment?

Can you begin to feel, see, hear your own truth? Can you begin to know that there is great purpose to your life, and that your inner being wants to shine brightly and share that purpose? It takes time; it takes trust; it takes being in silence. Not running. Listening. But that voice is in there, waiting for you to acknowledge it, waiting for you to own it and share it.

You are the creator of your own happiness. You are the master of your destiny, the captain charting your course. When we listen and align with our inner knowing, that voice, that crack of light, then things begin to shift, and the path becomes clearer and clearer.

We are all, no exception, shadow and light. It is only when we embrace our shadow side, as a mother would a child, that we fully love and accept our wholeness and share our light completely. We are each a million stars.

✑ Knowing

Sometimes, I forget how magical I am. How unique and important my contributions are. My existence is proof that there is something important for me to share. This is true for each of us. The only true limits are the ones in our minds. We are all fragments of the whole, all fractals of light.

Thought:

No one else can tell me just how far I can go; it's an open road. No questioning, just stepping one foot in front of the other, Trusting, knowing, that the next right step will appear.

I get to chart my course; I am my own hero.

We are receptors. And we buzz with the highest vibration when we are in touch with our inner knowing, our deepest truth. We can access and tap into our divinity, our direct line to Source. If you feel something in your body when you read this, then you know. You have the inkling. You remember. You sense that you are more than your body and mind. That there is a deeper energy flowing through you that is all of life that has come before and will ever be. A part of the Whole. You hear the nudge, the voice, you feel it deep in your bones, your truth. We have so much unexplored potential. Our lives are *endless possibility*. We can open to the magic. Give yourself permission right now, in this moment.

What is it you feel in your heart, in the quietest moments of the night? What is the longing you have, and what do you want to bring into your reality? What do you see yourself doing, sharing, *being* in your ideal life? All things are possible. *All things.* You must hold your vision intently in your focus. You must see those circumstances aligning in your mind's eye. You must hold the vision strong and clear, in great detail. It will manifest if you believe it to be so, if you accept that it is already done.

"You must believe it to see it."
–Dr. Wayne Dyer

✑ Gratitude

Turn around and face the sun, let it warm your soul, there is healing
to be found here, you have to know.
–From my song, The Healing

Over the last year, I've cultivated a practice of writing in my gratitude journal every day, noting things, people, circumstances for which I am grateful. It is a never-ending list, as infinite as the Abundance that exists for us. It's all in where you look, what you perceive, how you choose to see.

We have a choice. And our choice to see from a place of love is one of abundance. The choice to see gray and lack is one of scarcity. It is born of fear. Choose to see from love every step of the way, no matter what the external conditions are.

I am a messenger. I cannot tell you your truth. I cannot choose for you. I cannot sit in silence for you. You must create the opening, get a glimpse of your truth and want more of that. You must do the healing. You must access your light and bring it to the world in a big way. No one else can do it for you.

Choosing your truth is a daily practice. That crack of light, of seeing, of knowing, is the first step. You know the inner workings of your heart, and you know what brings you great joy. You know the whispers of your soul, the yearnings of your heart. Keep walking the path, following the crack of light. Pay attention to the little voice inside you, to the nudges you feel pointing you in a new direction. All the answers are inside of you. You decide how you see.

❦ CULTIVATION

We can cultivate an awareness.
We can cultivate a connection.
We can cultivate the life we most wish to live.
We can cultivate our gifts to share with the world.

We are one and the same energy as our higher power. We have a direct connection. We do not need anyone or anything else to directly connect with and cultivate Love; it is within us and around us always. We are God; God is us. All parts of the Whole.

Cultivating your alignment with Source, your higher power, whatever you name it, feels like *coming home*. Peaceful, warm, comforting. Good, right, a relief. You are exactly yourself, exactly where you want to be, rippling your peace outward to anyone who crosses your path.

✦ RESILIENCE

I can see now how I was so afraid of loss that it had a huge hold on me, a tight grip. But loss, change, and death are crucial parts of life, the human experience, and you can't truly live, experience life without it. Once you accept that and let go, you transcend the fear. That was a big one holding me back. All of the challenges bring us growth and to a better, more fulfilling place. I am grateful for the challenges that make me who I am, and I accept and open to growth and change. It is paramount to decide to stay the course and be okay no matter what.

Thought:

We limit our capabilities, our joy, our call.
When we choose to play it safe and stay small.
Your core star, your essence shines bright.
It wants to break free of the limiting vision
That your conscious mind can see.
Our choices perpetuate our reality.
What we believe, we see.

✋ DOING

So often we partake in the *doing.* The busy-ness. The stress and angst. The outcome. The lists. The heaviness.

Here is what the Divine Source wants: for us to *be.* To slow down. To witness the magic and wonder of the everyday. To breathe. To relax. To know lightness.

Yes, our human experience has challenges, pains, difficulties. These are opportunities for growth, for expanding our Being, for learning, for loving.

Can we maintain a stance of love, compassion, magic and light in the face of adversity?

Can we ask *What's next?* instead of *Why me?*

Can we see the positive aspects, the silver linings, in all of our circumstances, amidst all the tasks and frustrations and detours?

We are not victims. We are *beings of light.* If we can remember our divinity, there is only Love. Even when our lists are long.

✥ EXPANSION

Just as the Universe is constantly expanding, so is our nature. We are expanding, learning, evolving, eternally. To remain stagnant or small is to deny our very essence–in fact, the nature of all things!

We must go beyond our physical reality to glimpse the eternal nature of who we are. We are meant to be ever-evolving, expanding beings of consciousness. When we become fixed, we become hard, immobile, contracted.

It is important to note that *this* is when free will and choice come into play. When we experience an obstacle or challenge, which is a growth opportunity, we are meant to feel and process it. But then we have a choice: to stay in the grief/hardship/fixed mode or to mobilize and walk through the fire to the next phase of expansion.

Life is meant to be a journey, and we must continue moving forward. It does not do any good to always be looking back, to regret, to *what if*, to stop. That goes against the rules of our nature.

Sometimes our past tries to creep in, hold us back, keep us bound and frozen in place. Our ego can keep us small, anxious, cold. We often persist in this way out of fear, and if we can see it for what it is, we can choose differently. We can choose to align with love, warmth, growth.

Like a teeny plant emerging from the womb of a seed, we can keep growing, even when everything feels different from before. We can open and reach and strive and live and love.

Each of us is a microcosm of the Universe–so many stars, so much life force, so much expansion. We must not attach too heavily to our mind, our human form, but listen and be in our Knowing, which has been around forever and knows that it must, and longs to, continue to evolve.

This is our nature. We are the Universe.

❧ BREAKING OPEN

It was the summer of 2017, and my marriage was clearly unraveling. We had tried to patch things, attempted to connect, done couples counseling–we even considered an open marriage. But the thing is, when something is complete, it is complete. And no matter how much we want to control that or rail against it, the best thing we can do is surrender and let go.

I can honestly say that our time of separation was way more difficult for me emotionally than my breast cancer diagnosis. We had been together for more than 20 years and had two children together. Changing our family paradigm was very painful for both of us.

In the middle of this chaos and transition, I had the opportunity to travel to Italy with my lifelong best friend. We had dreamt of doing this together since high school, and our chance arose when one of her cousins in Italy was getting married. We turned it into a two-week trip together, along with her mother and sons, who are like family to me. It was an amazing golden treasure in the midst of a terribly difficult time in my life.

We would be staying with Onie's family in Santa Maria Capua Vetere, in the Province of Caserta outside of Naples. Her aunts and cousins were wonderful hosts; I could not keep track of how many times a day the espresso pot came around! The whole family was so welcoming to me. Though my Italian was rough, Onie was easily able to translate for us. After the wedding, which was like a storybook fairytale, Onie and I had planned to travel to the Amalfi coast for four days on our own. As the trip unfolded, my friend didn't feel comfortable leaving her mother and sons several hours away, so I decided to continue and take the side trip on my own.

I had booked the Airbnb six months prior, and I remembered virtually nothing about it. I hadn't even planned how to get there yet. It was just one of those quick decisions: *That one looks good, price is right, on the Amalfi coast, book it.*

The day arrives. Onie's cousin graciously drives me to the train which I take to Salerno, where I catch a bus to the Amalfi coast. I now need to find some way up the mountain to the small town of Pontone. Hours and hours of varied travel.

I get to the piazza in this small town (with too much luggage) and discover there are 200 steps up to the entrance to Palazzo Verone where I am to stay. Two hundred.

Luckily, the host has sent someone down to help me with my bags, and we ascend.

I arrive at the door, and I am greeted by a lovely woman who introduces herself as Bruna, Michele's wife. They own the B&B. Michele is at the market.

I walk into the main room, and it takes my breath away: There is a grand piano in the middle of the common room and four guitars set up along the wall. I think to myself, *Is this some kind of cosmic joke? What is happening right now? Where are the cameras? What are the chances?*

I didn't remember the Airbnb listing saying anything about a musician living there. But this was real. This was the Universe saying, *This is who you are. Live your truth.*

Michele arrived, and the two of us played music together (and we three became fast friends) over the next four days. Bruna was entirely gracious about our jam sessions and impromptu video recordings.

Michele and I still collaborate over technology. I set English lyrics to some of his compositions, and we've co-written four songs. We cheer each other on in our musical adventures. He is a true friend and a soul brother to me. Bruna and I share a special heart connection, too.

I am astounded by what unfolds when you decide to jump in, let go, and open up to what can be created.

Present day: My ex-husband and I are wonderful co-parents; I love him and wish him the best of everything, all the goodness life has to offer. He's happily remarried to a woman who is wonderful for him, and he for her. I couldn't be happier for him. And I am spending time exploring my own possibilities and cherishing my own heart.

At one point during our separation I told my ex-husband, "I don't want to be that couple in the supermarket in their 80s yelling at each other, calling each other names because *Those are the wrong kind of pickles, you idiot.* I just couldn't see the value or love in that.

And though our paths were separating, and it was excruciatingly painful, I trusted that our relationship would be better off in the end.

Co-parents. Uncoupled. And still friends.

♪ CLEARING

This is a journey, and you are ever-evolving. There is no destination or endpoint. Only growth, expansion, eternity.

Any resistance you feel to your evolution will create hardship, struggle, limitations, disease, and strife. When you trust the process, the Knowing, struggling will cease. Aligning with Source allows you to see the bigger picture.

I am a believer.

There have been so many times in my life when sitting and opening to the writing (for me, mostly at my piano) was a healing and spiritual experience.

I see now that our words can serve us, and our words can block us. Same goes with our thoughts.

If we speak and think from a place of love and positivity and light, it will bring us to a new level of understanding and peace.

To get to that love and positivity, writing out any thoughts of anxiety and clearing out the resistance that blocks us can be an important step.

Clear the path, get rid of the noise and the clutter in our heads, and watch the magic unfold.

✆ Alignment and Creating

Do we create? Do *we* create? Or are we *co*-creating? Are we stepping into alignment with the force, the energy that creates all matter since the beginning of time?

Our thoughts and our emotions create our experience. Vibrations constantly shifting–rising, lowering, becoming clearer or filling with static.

And so it serves us, when we are in creating mode and at our closest to Source/God/Magic, to sit and listen, to follow the nudge, our gut, and tap into the powerful creation energy that is here for us always.

Plug in.

That whisper, that nudge, that idea, that spark you feel . . . follow *that*. No one has created before the thing that you uniquely bring to this energetic life experience. Follow your heart, your gut, your *joy* to the place of unique creation, the story that only you can bring forth and share with the world.

✿ I Am Here. I Am My Own Hero

We each have this kernel of truth, of beauty, of who we really are. Sometimes, it's nurtured and grown; in the right conditions, it flourishes. That kernel opens up, becomes a flower, raises its beautiful face to the sun and the sky and proudly declares, "I am here. I am beautiful. I am one of a kind. I am divinity."

But sometimes the kernel is not watered, not nurtured. It doesn't get a chance to grow or bloom, to develop fully into itself. It is kept guarded, small, hard–and it feels safe. But that tiny kernel will not know the feeling of the sun on its leaves or the warmth of what could be.

If we are still in kernel form, we don't have to wait for someone else to remember that we need care. Our willingness to see and love ourselves can bring us to life, can nullify any past experiences or fears, and can give us the courage to unfold, bloom and bask in the glow of our personal truth, our unique glory.

Life is surely messy. We learn as we go. We forget who we are. But there is no right or wrong; there are choices. We can course correct at *any* time. We can choose differently if we want a different outcome.

It's like Glinda told Dorothy in the Wizard of Oz: "You've always had the power, my dear. You just had to learn it for yourself."

You have it within you. The power to return home. The ability, the strength, the love, the knowing. No matter what has come before, it is eternally within you, your truth.

You can be your own hero.

✤ Habits

If you continue to see things as they currently are, they will persist. If you choose to see the possibilities, to see what can be, transformation is set in motion. What we choose to think about is what will be created in our experience; it becomes our reality. Energy moves toward visualization.

And we can tend to have a limited vision, awareness, scope of what is really possible. It's like we forget to keep our dreaming and imagination muscles in shape. When we reawaken our imagination to all that can be, our possibilities are endless. Infinite. Expansive.

When we accept responsibility for our own happiness, we can release what has held us back, and we can move forward into our natural and blissful state of growth and change. Look around you. Nature does not hold herself back. Every spring, there will be new growth and the promise of more joy to come. In autumn, she seeds and looks forward to the changes and growth to come.

Trust that your natural state is happiness and enjoyment of the human experience. Trust in your daily gratitude for what is present. Trust that you can be, do and have anything you envision, and start today: Create a new picture for yourself, an imagining of what you want your life to be. You will be awed by how quickly the shifts begin to take place to support your vision, if you let it feel real, if you create a new habit of visualizing possibility.

✎ Soup

I love how organic life is. It's like making a homemade soup and then sitting down to enjoy it. Mindfully, lovingly putting together the ingredients as an act of love and joy, and then enjoying that meal, all the nutrients blended together, all the flavors mixing beautifully. Even if it's a flavor you've never tasted before, it somehow also feels as familiar as a warm hug or your favorite pair of shoes.

You pick your ingredients carefully, choose just the right olive oil, select the right herbs and spices based on your experiences, your desires. You combine them and you let them simmer. You may add more of one spice or another, tasting as you go. It simmers together, warming to just the right temperature. And then you have this most beautiful soup, and hopefully you are continually making soup, continually exploring new flavors on your journey.

No two soups are alike! We get to choose what ingredients will be in our soup, and what we will exclude. We get to choose whether it's a broth or a cream, whether it's complex or simple, whether it's a gazpacho or a hot soup. The beauty and the joy comes in choosing: choosing your ingredients, choosing to amend the recipe along the way.

What will *your* soup taste like? It's so much fun to sit back and think about all the ingredients, all the flavors, all the possibilities you get to choose from. *And* you get to pivot in the middle of the process to add whatever you want to! You get to add, amend, evolve at any point.

This soup–your soup–is meant to be enjoyed. It's meant to be consumed. It's meant to be a blissful and exciting adventure. I hope you enjoy not only making your soup, but consuming it, experiencing it, letting its warmth fill your entire body.

✑ GUIDANCE FROM THE SPIRIT REALM

I do receive "messages," I guess you can call them. Sometimes in words, sometimes in song. I have to be very open and very still to hear the messages. When I am open and listening, I can discern the name of the spirit entity when they impart insights. I want to share some of these with you, to be of some comfort:

Joy (Mary)
Joy is your birthright. Joy is key to calibrating to your highest vibration, to manifesting your ideal, most beautiful life experience. Tapping into and experiencing joy, we can immediately feel the connection, the alignment, our true nature. We are meant to fly, to laugh, to dance, to feel all of the amazingness of this experience.

Ride your bike down a big hill, squealing with delight. Allow your childlike spirit out to play. Stop being so serious. Stop making it harder than it has to be. Joy is a direct line to Source, to love, to peace within. Know your joy, experience your joyful spirit, and have *fun*. Include what lights you up, what you love, every day in your life.

Declutter (Jobe)
Declutter. Remove those objects, circumstances, people from your experience that weigh you down, who don't believe in you, that are negative. Lighten your load.

Declutter. Remove those things that cause you anguish, hardship, angst, heartbreak. Allow only for the circumstances and conditions of the highest vibration in your vortex. Be vigilant about protecting your energy.

Declutter. Your space, your surroundings, must be light. Sunlight and airflow are important. Nature is important. Align with the lightness of your being, and your physical circumstances will naturally follow.

Declutter. Let fresh air in. Breathe the lightness.

Quiet (Frieda)
Rest, relaxation, rejuvenation–these are all important to keeping your energy strong, vibrant, shimmering. Taking a break and just sitting–letting your mind quiet, your soul wander, and your heart revel in the down time–is key to our well-being.

Reading, sitting in meditation, resting your body (napping midday!), unplugging from media and devices, getting into nature, slow deep breathing–these are all ways for you to rest, to allow your soul to relax.

It is necessary, in order for you to do your important work. You must be able to rest, protect your energy, and refill your well, so that you can bring forth your best, brightest light to shine.

Love (Geoffrey)
When you are your most true, high-vibration self, you attract high-vibration, like-minded people to join you on your journey, either temporarily or for the duration. Not everyone who intersects with you at the high level of vibration will remain with you always. Sometimes you cross paths to help each other on the journey for a short while.

Real love, true love, is about nonattachment. It is about freedom, not control. It is about a living and breathing, morphing experience and is not meant to be locked down and stagnant. Real love allows the other person to be who they are, in any moment, as we are all constantly evolving. Lucky and blessed are those who can evolve together and allow space for each other to grow, uninhibited.

Love of the deepest kind, is not necessarily romantic love, though it can be. It is seeing the other person deeply, on a soul level, for who they are, and loving them through the messy, hard parts, and being willing to listen to them, to really see them.

This includes self-love! Loving yourself means allowing your evolution, allowing yourself to be seen and heard, allowing yourself to embrace both the challenges and the magical gifts on your journey.

✿ As Is

Here's the thing: You exist, you are, you *be*. That's all you need. Your *being*. That's enough. That means you are worthy, valuable, valid. You are unique and have a purpose in this world.

You are enough. Just you. Today. *As is.*

You can quiet any voices, internal or external, that have you doubting yourself, or loathing yourself, that tell you that you aren't good enough, or that the things you see and desire are not possible.

You can tune out that static, the noise of those detrimental messages, and focus on one thing only:

I am enough, and I get to create and experience the life I'm born to live.

Remind yourself of that daily, even several times a day, until you internalize it and believe it in your cells.

❧ New Beliefs

When we understand that our limiting beliefs are not relevant, and we decide that we are worthy of transformation and love and abundance, then it's time to dance! To reclaim your power, to visualize your ideal life with clarity, and to instill *new* beliefs and pathways.

After we unearth the lies, the obstacles, the limiting beliefs that hold us back (often self-imposed), we get still and we get clarity so that we can take action!

Meditation:

I leave behind all of my old ways of being, my old life, my limiting beliefs, and I step into my magnificence and power. I step into the new me, today. I release any resistance I feel to embodying my greatness, and I welcome in well-being and love. I align with my truth, my highest good, my source of joy. Miracles? I expect them. I let go of resistance, and I invite in goodness and light. Well-being and abundance. Nothing holds me back, and everything is in alignment. I step into my truth, and I embody the expansive, amazing life that is mine. I launch my vision and my new life.

✆ CONNECTION

The heart-to-heart connection that we all desire, the shared human experience, it's right here. We think we are separate, but we are all very much of the same creative energy and light, of love.

Small children know. They get it. Everyone is a friend, and there are no barriers or differences (unless outside influences are at play).

We owe it to ourselves and our children to encourage connection, to remember that the only barriers are those in our mind, and that perception and beliefs create our reality.

Unlearning is possible. Replacing with a new mindset is possible. Reprogramming neural pathways is possible. Our inherent nature is oneness with the whole. That connection, that love, never dies. It is there for you still, and always.

❦ VIBRATION

There is something so magnetic and healing and grounding to me about the frequency of the vibration of middle C, the B below and the D just above. Those vibrations, those tones resonate in my gut and remind me that I too am vibration, that I am alive and ever-changing, a pulsing energy, and that all of reality is vibration.

I am light; my essence is joy and love and light. That is the essence of each of us, the perfection and magnificence of our beings, today. In this moment.

Sometimes you need to wait and listen—to tune in to the vibrations of your highest self, your inner knowing.

Like the most active, right thing you can do is:

Be still, be open, *be.*

✸ The Door Will Open

We are not perfect: We all make mistakes. We all experience fear at some point. We all seek to love and be loved. (Our similarities *far* outweigh our differences!)

Even though I don't experience perfect joy all the time, I do know that the more aligned I am with Source, with my own divinity, the happier and more effortless my experience becomes. The source of all creation is goodness and light and wants us to be happy and live our joy, our purpose.

There is another plane of existence, that more and more people are accessing and aligning with. Here, there is no work to be done–only following your joy. Doing what makes you truly happy and fulfilled. Living your truth and letting go of people, circumstances, beliefs that no longer serve.

Source is expanding, but it is also constant. Always here, never ending. Always here for *you*.

Trust that each step toward your *self*, your truth, your *home*, leads to the next right step. The door will open.

✑ RELEASE

I was born when I turned 50. I suppose re-born may be more accurate. It is when I birthed myself into *being* who I truly want to be, or accepting who I always truly was. I finally allowed myself to live with integrity, embracing and honoring my truth and my path.

My cancer diagnosis led me to give myself that permission, *finally*. To live out loud and how I wanted to live. To wake up in a profound and life-changing way.

I imagine the main reason we can stay so buried and disconnected is in response to tragedies large and small–real pain, trauma, fear. But I believe that disconnection from our true selves is the actual tragedy. It's not so much the pain or loss we go through; the real tragedy occurs when we don't process the pain, the origin wound, when we don't allow ourselves to move beyond that pain, to grow and experience life and love from a place of truth. The tragedy is burying our hearts and our light.

Often, we're too young to know how to survive or cope otherwise. If the adults around us aren't aware and don't model emotion processing, then we can stay buried, fearful and lost for many, many years. In some cases, a whole human lifetime.

I want you to know, my friend, that it is never too late to process and heal a heart wound, and step into your true life, your life of great love, joy and positivity.

Is it work? Well, yes, in a manner of speaking. You'll need to open that wound, connect to that experience, feel the emotions in a safe environment, and then let it *go*. You'll need to trust that the healing and the best life is waiting for you on the other side of your pain. You'll need to have emotional support in place (a professional is advised) as you release your trauma.

But the bottom line is, at any point in your experience, you *can* choose. You can choose to release the past, to see the light and joy, the love, the glass half-full. You can choose change, healing, and growth . You can choose to see your beauty, your value and your importance.

I am living proof that a trauma held for more than 40 years can be released, that there is nothing to fear. It is pain, it is emotion, it is healable.

You, too, can release long-held fear and resistance that keeps you disconnected from love, joy and expansion. You, too, can make new choices. You can choose to see the beauty in what you experience every day, while you open to the goodness and love that is waiting for you.

You are worthy.

ENCOURAGEMENT

Self-love is non-negotiable.

Be kind and gentle with yourself.

Forgiveness has a part to play in every story.

We are a work in progress, always.

Our experience is the sum of our choices; at any moment we can choose differently.

It's okay to let the tears flow, and wash away your sadness.

Take alone time, to listen and be in stillness.

Trust your joy, follow your heart and passion.

Play is more important than work!

We are beings of ease, not struggle.

You can let go of who you thought you were, and re-create/imagine who you want to be.

Ask your higher power for guidance, on any topic.

Ask your guardian angels for love and protection.

Your story is important.

Your life is valuable.

You are worthy.

About The Author

Photo by Michael Lowe

Karen Novy is a songwriter, performer, vocal empowerment coach, author and speaker. She believes deeply in the healing power of music, has seen it touch many hearts and lives, and is dedicated to being an unstoppable force for love and healing in the world.

In the past year, Karen Novy wrote and launched her one-woman show, "A Hero's Journey: Coming Home," an inspirational performance piece that is one part storytelling, one part songtelling.

She also facilitates group vocal empowerment workshops, incorporating elements of sound healing and writing to help participants express and empower their voice. This is her first book.

You can find Karen's music on iTunes, Amazon and Spotify. Contact Karen through her website KarenNovy.com/connect. Email dragonflymusicllc@gmail.com to book vocal empowerment workshops, speaking engagements, performances and book readings.